YOU
are the
Vibe

Your Guide to Getting Out of Your Head,
Into Your Power, & Growing From Within

YOU
are the

*Your Guide to Getting Out of Your Head,
Into Your Power, & Growing From Within*

ERICA KNOLL

To everyone who is ready to reintroduce themselves
to the world…

This one's for you.

noun

---

a general feeling or sensation that someone gets or has about something

the character, quality or atmosphere of a place, situation, etc.

connection; rapport[1]

verb

---

be compatible; be in agreement or harmony[2]

1 "Vibe, Noun (1, 2, and 3)." Dictionary.com. https://www.dictionary.com/browse/vibe.
2 "Vibe, Verb (7)." Dictionary.com. https://www.dictionary.com/browse/vibe.

Contents

Foreword

As I sit here and write this I can't help but be transported back to several years ago when a bright, courageous (yet slightly terrified) woman popped into my messages. There was something about her…energetic. Eager. I could feel, even through just a few conversations, that she was on the edge of some big life changes.

I remember it so clearly. She told me how the vision she had for her life was "blurry and vague." She then went on to say she was a "quarter-to-half believer in all the spiritual, higher power, universe stuff." My oh my, how things have taken a turn.

If you haven't already guessed, yes, I'm talking about Erica. The woman who has so bravely taken charge of her own life, reclaimed her power, found her voice, and is paving the way forward into what's actually possible for people when they decide to start living for themselves *first*.

I had the honor of working closely with Erica for about two years as her life coach. During our work together I watched her as she healed, grieved, outgrew friendships, dove deep into emotions and feelings that had been suppressed for years, took charge, learned to use her voice, embraced the unknown over and over again, found love, and came fully into the understanding of what it meant to not only build the life of your dreams but *become the woman who can hold it all.*

It's funny how the universe works. In many of my sessions with Erica she would tell me how much she had always thought about writing a book. We even brainstormed one day on what topics she could write on. We never did land on that topic or create the clarity for her book during our work together, as there were other pieces of her life that were asking for attention. But now, looking back, I know exactly why the pages of this book poured through her when they did.

She needed to walk this path. She needed to come full circle and see the lessons to completion, appreciate how far she has come and root into the pieces, processes, tools and shifts that got her here—all of which are housed inside of this book. The universe had a plan for her all along, but she had to get here on her own. So here we are.

You are the Vibe feels like it's an old friend talking straight to you. But not the kind of friend who sugarcoats or gives you a bunch of fluffy advice. This is not another personal development book pumped up with fancy, spiritual lingo that you won't understand written by someone on their pedestal looking down telling you what you *need* to be doing to change your life.

Erica shares her story in a way where you're going to see so many versions of yourself throughout her journey. She speaks about the things many of us face off with but don't have the courage to say out loud. Her transformation speaks through the pages of this book and you can literally feel that her core desire in writing this is to support others through the very transformation she has walked.

As you will soon see, these pages aren't filled with a bunch of concepts that leave you feeling inspired but with little to no action plan. This book is rooted in action, tangible steps, processes that actually work, and grounded guidance from someone who started out, probably very much like you and me, not knowing what the hell she was doing but kept trusting that there was more for her to find, do and *be*. Each chapter takes you on a little ride, allowing you to feel seen, held, and validated in your feelings, but also calling you forward into what you're capable of.

If you've hit a roadblock within your own personal growth, have been feeling the pull towards making some big life changes, and want to start creating momentum towards what's truly possible for you, you've landed in the right place.

Erica's got you. Every step of the way. And I have to say that the quarter-to-half believer who was on the fence about this "stuff" and had a blurry vision of what she wanted her life to be has become a full-blown embodiment of what it means to live a life of alignment, integrity, and leadership. As Erica says…

"You have the power to change your story at any given moment."

Now it's your turn.

Keri Kugler
Certified life coach, business mentor, and host of the
Aligned Woman Podcast

Introduction

Picture This…

You're in elementary school and the teacher asks a question. You think you know the answer, but you don't raise your hand and you pray she doesn't call on you because then you have to speak out loud…and what if you're wrong? How embarrassing.

You're in middle school and your friends are talking about boyfriends. You're just sitting there anxious, hoping they don't say anything to you because you have little to no experience in that department and you feel like a loser.

You're in high school and you hop on every fashion trend possible, because you think it makes up for the fact that you're not all that pretty.

You're in college and you feel so out of place because everyone is having fun and experimenting with new things, but you're the good girl and don't do any of that.

You finally get that boyfriend and you think it'll last forever; you think it *should* last forever so you stay for twelve years… even when you know you're both too comfortable and your values don't align.

You move on and end up staying in a toxic relationship for two years because you've falsely convinced yourself things will get better, and you really don't want to be alone again.

You realize your whole life you've just kind of existed. You weren't bullied, but you weren't cool. You weren't a loner, but you didn't have a ton of friends. You were…just there. Just there letting your anxiety, lack of confidence, and limiting beliefs about yourself run the show. This is just who you are.

Does any of this sound even remotely familiar? Do/did you ever feel like this yourself? If so, welcome! I'm happy to have you; you've come to the right place!

Every single scenario above was a version of me I never truly understood or cared for. I couldn't fathom why I wasn't like other people. Why wasn't I more outgoing? Why was I so afraid of public speaking? Why was small talk so scary? Why didn't I have a boyfriend until I was twenty years old? Why was I so against breaking out of my comfort zone? Why did I constantly compare myself to others? Why did I stay in situations I knew weren't good for me? Why wasn't I good enough? Question after question about myself as a woman.

You see, for as long as I could remember, my happiness was dependent upon others. I had low self-esteem, low confidence, and quite frankly a low outlook on life. With that mindset, the thought of being alone was scary as hell. In my eyes, it was the worst possible outcome. I had so much going for me too. On paper, my life was as successful as they come. I had a good childhood, got good grades and stayed out of trouble, went to college and got a teaching job, was financially stable, could afford my own place, and had the ability to travel; however, I still felt like if I wasn't with someone, if I didn't have someone to share it all with, I wouldn't ever be happy. Codependency at its finest.

So what did I do? I let my relationships dictate my happiness and in turn, attracted all the wrong projects…I mean people. I'm a giver at heart and it showed in the romantic relationships I had, as well as trickled into my friendships. I didn't realize it at the time, but I held the belief that if I wasn't needed, I wouldn't be liked. If I didn't prove my worth through helping, I wouldn't be enough. I was loyal to a fault. I enjoyed helping others, but it was never fully reciprocated and relationships became disserving. I lost myself in my relationships, or more accurately, I never knew who I was in the first place. For a very long time, fifteen years to be exact, I didn't do a damn thing about it. I figured that's just how I was, and these were just the relationships that were meant for me. I couldn't have been more wrong.

After a toxic breakup at the age of thirty-five, I decided I'd had enough. Something had to change. This just couldn't be the life I was meant to live. After bawling my eyes out one too many times, it hit me: I never once took the time to build a relationship with myself. Not once. I concentrated most on what I could do to help others and although I am now extremely proud of the loyal, caring person I am, it served as a debilitating weakness when stacked on top of a wobbly, broken foundation.

This realization came in 2020, mere days before the Covid lockdown hit. With nothing else to do and nowhere else to go, I thought…what better time to go all in on me? I signed up for a virtual women's workshop and my journey to self-love began.

If you're feeling anything like I was, this book is for you. Here you'll find tangible steps you can take to shift your mindset, learn to love yourself, and create the fulfilling life you've always wanted. Jump in! Let's go for a ride!

Chapter 1:
Love Yourself First

First bit of hard truth: it all begins with you. I've learned firsthand that nothing changes if nothing changes. You cannot expect your life to evolve if you're not willing to look at the relationship you have with yourself. I'm going to guess that if this book sparked your interest, you're ready for some serious growth…you're ready to become the person you think only exists in your dreams. Well then, it's time to get uncomfortable and look inward. It's time to solidify your foundation, one crack at a time. Oh, and spoiler alert, that person you want to be already lives in the real world…in your real world. Let's get you loving yourself so you can trust and believe that.

Solo Dates

There are many things that have worked for me in regards to learning to love myself, but the number one thing I did was start taking myself out on dates. Why is this number one? Because learning to enjoy your own company physically teaches you to love who you are. You wouldn't want to hang out with someone you didn't like, so you need to stop putting yourself in that category. Doing activities solo was always built up in my mind as something extremely scary. Impossible even. All of the limiting beliefs you could possibly think of would run through my anxious mind:

I'm going to look like such a loser.
People are going to stare at me.
What if I see someone I know?
Will it look like I have no friends?
Everyone will know I'm single.
I'm too introverted to do something this bold.
I just can't do it.

The list could go on and on. Full disclosure: there was no chance I was far enough along in my journey to know how to work through and heal from those thoughts. What I did know how to do at that point was start small and do it anyway.

If you want your life to change, you need to change your life.

So for day one, I went for a quick breakfast at an outdoor restaurant and then walked to the beach. The beach is a perfectly acceptable place to be alone, right? What I found on this triumphant day was that the only person who was worried about me being alone…was me! No one else cared, and you'll find more often than not that this is the case in most scary situations.

That day led to lunch at a small local cafe, which led to meals at bigger establishments, which led to solo vacations. Each time I did something on my own it got less and less frightening. I started to realize that my fear of doing things alone was overpowering my ability to see how awesome I really was. The more I enjoyed my own company, the less my mind was anxious and I was able to be present in the moment. Now—because I still make it a point to take myself on dates to this day–it is liberating, and it feels so good to love spending time with my favorite person…me!

Your Turn

Where can you take yourself and just BE? Where is your favorite place to go? How can you start small and take yourself on a date?

____

____

____

____

____

Celebrate Yourself

If you're anything like me, you've spent a lot of time criticizing yourself. Wondering why you are the way you are or why you're not like others. Telling yourself stories about how this is just the way you are, while self-defeating thoughts run through your head:

Why can't I be more outgoing?
I'll never have that kind of confidence.
I'm just not that kind of woman.
I'll always be seen as the good girl.
I wish I looked more like her.
I wish I had her energy.
This is just how I am.

Any—or all—of those sound familiar? Here's the thing:

You have the power to change your story at any given moment.

We are all predisposed to qualities and core values that may feel out of alignment with who we truly want to be, but we're never stuck. We're never forced to be someone we're not. I guarantee that you have way more to offer this world than you give yourself credit for. My guess is that you wouldn't have picked up this book if you weren't in a place of wanting a shift. In order to get there, you're going to have to celebrate the crap out of the amazing person you are!

Think about where you are in life right now and how hard you've worked to get there. Think about the obstacles you've overcome. Think about that new job you got or that promotion you've earned. Think about the challenges you've faced and the healing you've done. Think about the relationships you've walked away from and those you've gained because you knew you deserved better. Think about the sheer fact that you are currently working on becoming the best version of yourself. There is so much worth celebrating once you really start acknowledging all that you are.

The first time I really took the time to write down my celebrations, the amount that I came up with blew my mind. Some crucial things I celebrated at that time:

- Leaving that toxic relationship.
- Investing in myself (more on that later).
- Shifting my mindset around grief and guilt.
- Learning to be happy alone.

I used to think that the small things weren't worth recognizing, but all of those experiences that seem minor or insignificant in the moment are the ones that lead up to big changes, so don't discount them. Acknowledge even the smallest of things daily: moving your body, cleaning your space, taking a baby step toward your goal, completing a task you've been putting off, maintaining a boundary, spending time with yourself, quality time with friends and family, etc. Being in this state of celebration and gratitude will attract even more of it into your life.

Your Turn

List any and everything you can celebrate TODAY:

____

____

____

____

____

List any and everything you can celebrate from the last
THREE MONTHS:

____

____

____

____

____

List any and everything you can celebrate from the last SIX
MONTHS:

____

____

____

____

____

List any and everything you can celebrate from the last
YEAR:

____

____

____

____

____

____

Watch your mindset and perception of yourself shift when you truly see how exceptional you are. Time to celebrate!

| THE LESSON |

Learning to love myself gave me a new outlook on life, love, and friendships. I realized that I didn't need anyone else to make me happy, and I certainly didn't need to constantly try to fix people either. I granted myself the permission to be unapologetically me; no strings attached. I was ready to let go of anyone and anything that was no longer serving me and create the best life possible. For the first time in my life, I knew I was going to be okay, no matter what the future held. That mindset right there was the ultimate goal. What I once thought "would never happen for me" was happening right before my eyes, and the evidence couldn't be denied. I was strengthening my foundation one crack at a time…and I was ready for more.

Are you ready for more?

Chapter 2:
Invest in Yourself

I have found that the best way to dive into this type of inner work is to get help and learn from others. Going to therapy and hiring a life coach have without a doubt changed my life for the better. They both helped me in different ways, so you have to think about which approach you prefer or if you want both like me.

Therapy vs. Coaching

Let me start off by saying there is no shame in asking for help. If it were easy to do alone, you'd already be where you want to be.

You do not need to have "something wrong with you" to benefit from therapy or coaching.

These professionals are here to guide you and give you new, fascinating perspectives. I certainly wouldn't be the woman I am today if not for both.

In my experience, therapy benefited me greatly when I needed to work through a specific situation with logic, science, and tangible how-to's. Most recently I went to therapy as a means to learn how to cope with my relationship at the time, and to give me the strength to walk away if things didn't get better. This was that two-year toxic relationship I previously mentioned. When the breakup finally happened, I stayed in therapy to get over it and get myself to a point of being able to move on. Therapy got me in the position to be ready to work on myself; to be able to put him behind me and focus on building myself back up.

Coaching provided me with similar logic and how-to's, but also incorporated a spiritual aspect along with mindset work. This combination was pure magic. Shortly after therapy ended, I got a message from a coach I had been following on Instagram to join a free week-long challenge she was hosting. I thought, "Why not?" I had been investing so much time already into personal development and finding what works for me, so I didn't have anything to lose. I completed the challenge and her style of coaching really resonated with me. It felt as though she was always talking directly to my soul. This challenge led me to try one of her course offerings, which gave me a true taste of her coaching because it had a live group component. That course then led to a free consultation call to see if private coaching was right for me. From there I invested, and we worked together for close to two years. Life-changing is an understatement! She became a rock in my healing and evolution as a woman. Oh, and she wrote the foreword for this book! Thanks Keri!

Options Galore

I know what you might be thinking here: "But Erica, I don't have the money to pay for therapy or coaching." I see you. I was lucky enough to have insurance cover my therapy sessions, but I didn't immediately jump into finding a coach. The thought of spending that kind of money to work with someone I didn't even know scared me and brought out my skeptical side…the one that always had questions and wondered if things were too good to be true. What if we weren't an energetic match? What if it's a scam? What if I can't do the work correctly or it doesn't work for me? So I started small, and you can too. Maybe therapy and coaching are in your future, maybe they're not, but here are some other ways you can invest in yourself without breaking the bank.

Podcasts

Podcasts are such a valuable, free tool. There's something for everyone. One for every topic under the sun and all different lengths of time. Find one to three people that really resonate with you and give their shows a listen. You don't need a lot of time to be moved.

Podcasts have inspired some of my most crucial decisions: deciding enough was enough in getting over an ex…deciding there was more available for me and I was going to find it… deciding to write this book.

> **There is something so empowering about deciding, and oftentimes one thought, phrase, or sentence is all it takes to hit your heart and help you decide.**

Books

Personal development books are another great way to gain information and jumpstart your journey. I love them because I like to highlight important concepts I want to come back to in the future. And I don't know about you, but I love a good hard copy of a book!

Free/Inexpensive Offerings

Many coaches, influencers, course developers, etc. cater to a variety of budgets which means they'll have some offerings that are inexpensive or even free of charge. Look into this and utilize their knowledge. When you're just starting out, this is a great way to figure out what you like and what resonates with you. There are endless amounts of inspirational information out there, but it's not going to hit everyone the same way.

You need to find what speaks to your soul. What lights you up and moves you. What guides you toward embodiment.

Community

In addition to offerings such as masterclasses and courses, many people have a community, usually on Facebook, that can be joined for free. This gives you the opportunity to connect with like-minded individuals on a similar path as you. Take a look around and see where you think you'd fit in most. Community is a beautiful thing.

I made this a separate category because finding a community doesn't just have to be virtual or from social media. There are several different meet-up apps and sites you can look into, leagues you can join, or classes you can take. In doing so, you'll meet people who have similar interests as you even if they're not on the same journey as you. That's okay!

My first real experience with community came when I joined a hatchet throwing league–yes, my little 5'1" self throws axes–by myself! It was one of the scariest things I had ever done and also the most fulfilling. It was 2018 and I was stuck in a rut. Everything felt so mundane and I just couldn't break out of my funk. I had done hatchet throwing before and it was fun, so when I saw they were creating a league I had an "ah-ha" moment. No one I knew wanted to join with me, so after trying really hard to talk myself out of it and claim it was too scary (because that's what I always did)...I joined! I didn't know a single person, including my partner who was chosen for me. When I got there I wanted to vomit and leave immediately (which I didn't, thank goodness!). Being social and meeting new people is something that never came naturally to me, so this was way beyond my comfort zone. It was a little awkward at first and it took a bit for me to find my place, but once I did it was one of the most amazing feelings. I'm happy to say that I'm still doing it to this day, and I still deem it the best thing I ever did for myself. The people that I met are some of the greatest people I know, many of whom have become dear friends of mine, and after three years of being in the league, I met the love of my life. I don't think it's possible for me to be more grateful for this community. All because I took a step. I took action. I went outside the box. I did the scary thing. There is usually sheer greatness on the other side of your comfort zone.

Who you surround yourself with–virtually or in your physical circle–matters, and there is no better feeling than having a supportive community.

The key with all of these things is to not do too much at once. There is such a thing as overdoing it in the personal development world. Don't try to listen to ten different podcasts, read book after book, and join every opportunity on the market. You'll wind up overwhelmed and stuck in a state of inaction.

If you're looking to hire a coach at some point, and I highly suggest you do, don't take advantage by finding several and trying to utilize every possible free or inexpensive tool you can. That again will be overwhelming and lead to inaction. Focus on one or two that seem to vibe with what you're working toward and check out their offerings. Look for what truly speaks to you and progress from there. If it's not a match, move on. If you think it could be, connect and find out what would be best for you.

Your Turn

Identify what type of learner you are–visual, auditory, or both. This can determine which type of tool might work best to get you started. If you're a visual learner, make a list of three books that seem to speak to the path you want to walk. If you're an auditory learner, list three podcasts and audiobooks. If you're both, combine those lists.

Look at your list and circle one book (after this one of course) and one podcast you want to start with. Add the others as you see fit, but remember, if you start to feel overwhelmed, dial it back. Dive deep into what's resonating. There is no rush.

Make a list of your hobbies. What do you LOVE to do? Write any and everything, big or small.

Circle three that you enjoy most. How can you utilize them to find or build a community? (i.e. post more about them on social media, find Facebook groups around these interests, find local leagues, attend live classes, etc.)

____

____

____

____

____

____

| THE LESSON |

If you can afford therapy and/or a coach, do it! Go all in and watch your life change drastically. However, there are endless possibilities and tools when starting (and continuing) the personal development journey. In order to combat the feeling of being overwhelmed, only utilize what works for you. Don't worry about what you think you *should* be doing. Focus on what makes you feel empowered. Over three years ago, I started with the book *You Are A Badass* by Jen Sincero and Sarah Ordo's *Her Best F***ing Life* podcast. I've now branched out to countless books and several podcasts, but I only read/ listen to what feels good.

If you don't vibe with it, don't use it. Period.

When it comes to community, try not to compare yourself to others. I was always jealous of the people who had big groups of friends. I wanted that because I thought it was the epitome of being cool. What I've come to learn is that less is more and quality is way more important than quantity. You can absolutely succeed on this journey alone. You do not *need* anyone, but it sure is fulfilling when you surround yourself with like-minded people. Ones who lift you up and support your growth. Ones who help you heal. Not any and everyone just to feel popular. So get out there and find your community… they're waiting for you!

Chapter 3: *Journaling*

I know, I know, journaling is such a cliché thing to suggest. Everyone already knows about journaling. Well, I'm here to take it beyond putting pen-to-paper. Sure, there are great benefits to writing things out, and we'll get to that in this chapter, but I want to start with something I like to believe I made up–verbal journaling. Audio journals exist, but in my case I'm not talking to a device or an app, I'm talking to myself. I talk to myself out loud so often that I find myself doing it in public, and need to remember that other people can see and hear me.

Verbal Journaling

It is extremely clarifying to take what's going on in your mind and express it verbally.

I do this just about every morning. It helps me clear my head and organize my thoughts. Whether it's my to-do list for the day or my mind is just racing, it helps me feel ready to take on the day. Mental clutter is a real thing and talking to myself regularly eliminates a lot of that.

In addition to my morning routine, verbal journaling helps me with decision-making. I've always told myself the story that I'm an indecisive person and because of that, I became an indecisive person. Funny how that works. Anyway, speaking out loud about all possible outcomes of a decision helps me make the best one. It helps me to expect the best (being the best-case scenario girl is still new to me), and acknowledge and prepare for the less desirable.

Another way I love to use verbal journaling is when writing is not an option. Are you ever in the car and something pops into your mind that really bugs you? Maybe it's something that just happened, or maybe it's something that you've been trying to heal from that keeps popping up. Driving is a prime time for me to have thoughts I didn't exactly ask for. In certain instances it's beneficial to simply redirect your thoughts, like saying no to the thought trying to invade your brain and thinking about something else instead. However we can't, and shouldn't, avoid it.

> **There's a difference between acknowledging and redirecting, and completely ignoring your thoughts and emotions.**

When redirection is not what feels good to me, I just start talking. I say out loud everything that is running through my mind. I even act out scenarios!

Here's an example from several years ago. I had a long-term friendship come to an end and although I knew it was the right decision, it was hard and took some time to heal from. Oftentimes when I was driving, I would think about the situation and get angry. Instead of festering in that anger, I spoke to myself and played out different scenarios. I defended myself. I took responsibility. I thought about what I would say if I ever spoke to her again. I acted appropriately and with integrity, but I also acted like a woman I didn't want to be, stooping to a level I wasn't aligned with (which felt kind of good to release, not going to lie). The thing is, I did this all out loud and to myself, which made the situation easier to deal with. It also made these emotional pop-ups more manageable, and in turn aided in my healing and moving forward.

This works for any situation and any emotion you might be feeling. It's liberating to release your thoughts from your mind and body and into the world–even if the world is just your steering wheel for the time being (side note: this works wonders in the shower too–where I think we all have our best and worst thoughts). Believe it or not, what we hold in our mind also gets held in our bodies. It takes up space and if it is not released in a healthy way, it will completely fill your vessel and overflow. Make space for the things you love instead of holding onto negative energy. Release, release, release!

Your Turn

What? Did you really expect lines to write here? Go talk to yourself!

Guided Journaling

Verbal journaling is definitely my favorite form, but there is also a time and place for written journaling and it's just as beneficial. When I first started journaling, I had the constant thought, "What do I even write about?" I felt like I was doing it wrong or that what I was writing about wasn't good enough. Fun fact: there is no wrong way to journal! Guided journals can help in this situation, and allow you to start your journaling process with ease.

The thing I love most about prompted journals is that you learn a lot about yourself. I started with *Mindful Makeover* by Stephanie Robilio. This is a question-a-day journal that walks you through what Stephanie calls The Magic Four: Awareness, Acceptance, Accountability, and Action. It is a wonderful thirty-day journal when you're just getting started and want to live more mindfully. I then moved on to *True You* by Kelly Vincent. This journal is beautiful and helped me dive deep into many aspects of my life that I never actively thought about: my values, identity, spirituality, and life purpose to name a few.

I'm giving you these examples because guided journals can hold so much power. We need to learn about ourselves in order to evolve.

Getting to know who you truly are allows you to become who you want to be.

We need to know where we stand on certain things, what triggers us, what needs healing, what we value most, and what we want. Learning these things–and I mean *really* learning them–is crucial because it also helps us to set boundaries for how we want to live our lives and what we are willing to accept for ourselves.

Your Turn

If interested in journaling, take some time to search for guided journals and see what stands out to you. Choose the one you like best, purchase it, and get started!

Mind Dumps

Mind dumps vary on the journal spectrum for me. They can be anything from writing about a specific topic to literally dumping all your thoughts onto the page. The point in all scenarios though, is to just write. Write whatever comes to mind. Write without overthinking.

> **This is the key to journaling: it doesn't matter what you're writing about or how you're writing it...just don't overthink it.**

An example of this would be when I was asked by my second coach, Sarah, to write down all the beliefs I held around success. Then she asked me what beliefs I *wanted* to have. This may not seem like a mind dump, but to me it was because I took it and ran. I wrote down every belief I could possibly think of and every belief I wanted in the future, even if it made no sense (no overthinking, remember?). I knew I'd get to re-read and make sense of it all with Sarah later. It's amazing what can come up when you stop overthinking and just write your heart out.

I also like mind dumps when something is weighing heavily on me and nothing else seems to work. If I've tried verbal journaling, redirection, sitting with my emotions, and everything in between and I don't feel that release, I mind dump. Whatever the situation is that I'm going through, I write down everything that's bubbling up. Every thought, every fear, every emotion.

In the more traditional sense, I have done mind dumps before bed to let go of any lingering thoughts that might keep me up at night. This is where there is no specific topic, question, or situation I want to write about. I just jot down anything that comes to mind. It could be about one thing or fifty, it doesn't matter. Turning off some of those thoughts through journaling helps calm your energy and prepare your mind for sleep.

Your Turn

Take some time and mind dump here. Write down anything that comes to you in regards to your emotions and the path you're choosing for your life. If you're having some trouble or feel nervous (totally normal if you've never journaled before), think about these:

What do you want to learn more about yourself?
Why did you buy this book? What do you want to work on?
What do you want your journey to look like?
What's holding you back?
What do you want most in life?

____

____

____

____

____

____

If you need more space, grab a notebook. Don't limit yourself… get it all out!

I want to end this section by clarifying that journaling can work for all things positive as well. I think as human beings, we focus a lot more on the negative aspects of life because those are what we need to work on healing. We think of this work (and journaling) as a means to combat trauma. While it's absolutely wonderful for that, it's also awesome for celebrating yourself, building your confidence, writing down your goals, and stepping into your power to claim what you deserve!

BONUS

Let's get positive! Answer any or all of the following questions:

What do you love about yourself?
What do you feel are your best qualities?
How would you describe yourself to someone who's never met you?
What are some of your accomplishments?
What are you proud of about yourself?
What are some of your talents?
What do you hope to offer the world?

____

____

____

____

____

Now go back and remind yourself what you've already celebrated from Chapter 1!

| THE LESSON |

Journaling doesn't have to be boring. You get to make it whatever you choose and do it however works best for you. The key is to not overthink it and be intentional. Know what you want to journal about, know what your goal is, and have fun. Journaling is something that should feel good…for your mind, body, and soul. It should help you work through tough times and celebrate yourself in good times. Make it a practice, not a chore.

Chapter 4:
Affirmations

If I was writing this book just a couple of years ago, I don't think this chapter would exist. I used to think affirmations were silly. How is saying or writing something that I don't actually believe about myself going to be helpful? I brushed the concept off for a bit, but then ultimately came back to it. As I moved along in my journey, I became more open minded; so, what could it hurt?

I started with affirmation cards. They came with a particular workout program I was doing, so I took advantage and pulled one each day. I read them, thought about how the message could relate to me and my feelings, left it visible for the day, and moved on. The ones I really liked I tacked to the wall where I kept the workout calendar. Unfortunately, this wasn't enough because I wasn't really embracing them.

> **When it comes to affirmations, you can't just read or say them and move on. Even when you don't fully believe them, if you don't find a way to embody them, they're essentially useless.**

After using the cards, I took it a step further by writing them on post-it notes and placing them around my apartment. I wrote a combo of "I am..." statements and ones regarding how I wanted to feel and what I deserved.

Some of my favorites included:

- I can find happiness in unexpected places.
- Settling is no longer an option.
- I deserve as much effort as I put out.
- I can't lose what is meant for me. (Courtesy of Cara Alwill; she said it on her podcast, *Style Your Mind*, and it has stuck with me ever since.)

Naturally, I placed a couple on my mirrors, but I also placed them in other areas I saw frequently: the front door, the refrigerator, and right by my bed. This placement led me to read them daily because they were all over.

I wrote these down with the main intention of finding love, but I also chose them because they all could trickle into other areas of life. They were universal and what I desperately wanted out of life. I wanted to live a more meaningful, joy-filled life. What initially held me back was that although I truly believed these were possible, I had zero evidence that they were possible for *me*. In my head they were all attainable and realistic, but my codependency conditioned me to believe happiness only came from intimate relationships. It conditioned me to believe everyone settles because no one is perfect and I have to do everything in my power to make it work. It conditioned me to believe that I'd always give more because that's just what I did. It conditioned me to believe I could lose anyone at any time and it would always be heartbreaking. It conditioned me to believe that what I wanted was asking too much or just flat out didn't exist.

But I had an open mind, right? So I posted them and I read them. Over and over. And then something magical happened. About a year or so later, when they had just become part of my decor and I wasn't reading them as actively as before, I read them one by one and guess what? They were all true… in my love life and beyond. I couldn't tell you when the shift happened–that's some behind the scenes universe stuff–but I can pinpoint some small moments that may have led up to this revelation:

- I learned to love myself and developed an immense amount of happiness around being single…unexpected, I know!
- I let go of settling for less than I deserved and deepened my friendships with those who lifted me up, showing me that there are others on my energetic level.
- I worked with my therapist and coaches to heal the trauma from my past and worked on letting go of what no longer served me in the present. This perspective opened my eyes to how I had never actually wanted what I lost long term…it certainly wasn't meant for me!
- I gained a sense of trust within myself when it came to romantic relationships, making me ready when love entered my world again and it has been glorious!

These types of action steps, the inner work, compounds over time. You go from a non-believer to starting to believe it could happen, to knowing your worth and what you deserve, to full-blown embodiment. And that right there is your power. That's the shift.

As time passed and I started to enter a new phase of change in my life, I needed an affirmation refresh. Instead of focusing on love, I wanted to focus on success. I had been exploring the idea of a career change, but kept telling myself it wouldn't happen for me. Here we go again, had I learned nothing? Rather than continue to tell myself this same story again and again, I jumped into immediate action…because if I have actually learned anything, it's that it *can* happen for me. Anything can happen for anyone. That's why I'm writing this book!

So I hired Sarah (a self-discovery coach who specializes in career changes and feeling stuck), started writing this book (a dream I've had for over ten years), leisurely explored possible opportunities, and revamped my affirmations. Here are the new ones I can't wait to see come to fruition:

- Everything is working *for* me.
- Money will continue to flow; I am meant for abundance.
- I am in charge of my thoughts, beliefs, actions, and energy.
- I can find success in unexpected ways.
- I am fulfilled in my career.

I kept some of the original affirmations as well because they made perfect sense for the intent of finding my new level of success. In total, I have seven affirmations to read daily and watch the magic unfold all over again. Chills!

Your Turn

Eight lines for eight affirmations—write down power statements that resonate with you. You can use mine as a guide, copy them entirely if they fit, or create some of your own. Remember, they can be "I am…" statements or they can hold an emphasis around what you want and deserve. There are no wrong affirmations. Have fun here!

THE LESSON

When you first start walking along this type of self-love path, it's extremely difficult to keep an open mind. At least it was for me. I held the mindset that "it'll never work for me" for so long that my instant reaction to all of this stuff was that it seemed a bit too out there for my liking. However, there was a part of me—a small part at the beginning—that knew I was meant for more; that knew my life could change for the better if I did the work. So I leaned into that part. I listened to that part and I'm so grateful I did. The dark clouds, the stories in your head, the fear…that's all going to stick with you for a while, but keep listening to the part inside you that wants more. The part that made you pick up this book. The part of you that feels this deep in your soul. The evidence will come, but you have to do the work as if you already know this.

Do the work and the changes you witness will be mind blowing.

Chapter 5:
Dance Parties (& Other *Confidence* Boosters)

Let's do a little *Your Turn* right off the bat:

When you think of the word confidence, what is the first thing that comes to mind?

____

____

____

____

____

For me, the first thing that always came to mind when I was younger was physical appearance. I never thought of myself as pretty, and therefore told myself I lacked confidence. I tried to make up for it by always being on top of the coolest trends. I wore cute clothes, accessorized, did my hair, and got my nails done. I thought it was helping at the time, but it was just a band-aid…a temporary fix to a problem that would haunt me for years to come.

That's because confidence is an inside job. It's the perfect combination of loving, trusting, and healing yourself. But perfect doesn't exist, so what do we do? We go deep. We look inside and we take baby steps. When you start looking at what is holding you back and hindering your confidence, it may feel like the blocks are caused by other people's opinions. Maybe you feel like you don't really fit in because you're not like them and *they* won't understand you. Maybe you don't speak up in a meeting because you're afraid *they* will think your comment is stupid. Maybe you don't tell your friend or significant other how you're really feeling because you're afraid *they* will get mad at you. Maybe you don't share certain things or show your face on social media because you're afraid *they* will think you're ridiculous. These are all prime examples of your confidence taking hit after hit, and these hits have nothing to do with physical appearance.

Oh, and these examples have all been me so just another friendly reminder that you're not alone here and you *can* make changes.

The glaring similarity in these four examples is the word *they*. Other people are responsible for your actions and feelings here so all you have to do is stop caring what others think… that's what *they* say, right? Not quite. The not-so-apparent pattern here is that your confidence actually has nothing to do with other people, and everything to do with what you think of yourself. You feel like you don't fit in because *you* tell yourself you don't and *you* aren't being your authentic self. You don't speak up in a meeting because *you* don't fully trust yourself to share a meaningful thought. You don't tell your friend or significant other how you're really feeling because *you* are afraid of losing them. You don't share certain things or show your face on social media because *you* worry you'll look ridiculous on a public forum. Do you see it now? It's much easier to blame others–even when it's not being done in a malicious way–but unfortunately, that's not going to make any changes or boost your confidence anytime soon.

You have to rewrite the stories you tell yourself so regularly. The stories that you've been telling for so long that you think there are no other possible stories. The stories that make you believe this is just who you are. It's not...you are *so* much more!

As you consistently work to heal, you'll begin seeing evidence that your confidence and trust in yourself are growing. What you'll also notice is that the "not caring what others think" will follow. That comes after–or even along with–doing the inner work first. And just to keep it real, I believe we all care what other people think and we always will–to an extent. When you're healing, however, everyone else's thoughts and opinions will drive your own actions and decisions much less. You'll be the one in the driver's seat, not *them*.

So why is this chapter titled "Dance Parties" you ask? Because kitchen dance parties are one of the things that boosted my confidence the most. It's silly I know, but it's silly in the best kind of way. Back in 2016, I started using some at-home workout programs. I had a friend whose girlfriend was one of the coaches for the company, so I signed up with her and began following her on Instagram. I would see posts of her and so many other coaches on her team doing pre-workout dance parties. My immediate thought when I saw this was, "That looks so fun. I could never do something like that on social media. I wish I had their confidence." Fast forward four years, and I myself became a coach. I gave it a try for a bit when the pandemic hit, but unfortunately it wasn't for me. It did, however, lead me to starting my own dance parties and for that I will be forever grateful. I remember posting my first one and being so scared of looking like a complete fool. But then I posted another and another and people started messaging me to tell me how much they loved them. If I didn't post one for a while, people even said they missed them. That was the proof right there that I was the only one judging what I looked like. Nine out of ten times no one cares as much as you do.

Not only am I still doing them now, but they have evolved so much since that first day. They've become inspirational dance parties. I choose a message or life lesson that feels aligned with me and a corresponding song, and I use it as a pre-workout hype up. Adding this kind of value to it lights me up inside, and I thoroughly enjoy sharing. Using my experiences and my words to inspire others is an ultimate goal for me—hence this book! On top of that, I no longer care if anyone thinks I look ridiculous. My dance parties are silly and uncoordinated, but instead of hiding them, I embrace all of them and just have an incredible amount of fun in the process. Confidence boost complete!

Of course dance parties are not the only way I've flexed my confidence muscle, and maybe dancing just isn't something you're interested in trying. Here are a few other tried and true things I've done over the past few years:

- Started speaking up for myself and communicating my feelings.
- Surrounded myself with people who encouraged me to be myself.
- Let go of what was no longer serving me.
- Hired two coaches.
- Made quicker decisions.
- Turned inward and got to know myself.
- Focused more on my self-care.
- Took myself on dates.
- Embraced an open mind.
- Wrote this book!

Some of these may seem vague, but that's because it looks different for everyone. What doesn't serve me, might serve you. My self-care might look different than your self-care. The point is, the more you focus on yourself, embrace who you are, learn to love yourself, and heal from the inside out…the more your confidence will grow.

> **Do the silly thing you've always wanted to do. Break out of your comfort zone. Try something new. Say no when you want to say no. Be yourself. Open up to the world authentically and watch how much you start attracting the people and things you never thought possible.**

Your Turn

After reading this chapter, does the word confidence take on any new meaning from what you wrote at the beginning? If so, what does confidence mean to you now?

What is something you have always wanted to do, but felt too shy or scared to try? Think about how you can make it happen!

What baby steps can you take to begin flexing your confidence muscle?

____

____

____

____

| THE LESSON |

Confidence has nothing to do with other people and everything to do with you. It's acknowledgement, it's healing, it's love, and it's learning to walk *with* your fear. Fear is inevitable and it often holds us back from being who we really want to be. That hurts our confidence because it makes us think we can't. Stepping out of your comfort zone doesn't just mean doing things scared. There are many things that scare us that we simply don't want to do. Growth comes when we don't let fear stop us from doing the things we truly *want* to do. This can be spiritual or physical. I'll end the same way I began–confidence is an inside job and you *can* continue to gain more by putting in the work!

Chapter 6: *Sit* With That

When I started working with Keri (my first coach) we would have these really powerful conversations that would spark new thoughts and ideas. The sessions would often end with her telling me to "sit with that and see what comes up." I wasn't honest with her right away, but I will be honest with you: I had no idea what that meant. I would just say okay, take a few minutes to "sit" throughout the week, and then move on because I was confused and felt like I was doing it all wrong. I finally flexed that confidence muscle again and asked her what it actually meant. I was always looking for the strict how-to action steps so naturally I asked how to do it properly, but moreover I wanted to know what she meant because I was taking it literally, just sitting in silence without any idea what to do. Her response blew my mind—not because of its complexity, but rather its simplicity. I couldn't believe how easy it was. She said:

"Ask yourself, 'How does it make me feel?'"

You're probably sitting there wondering why this is even a chapter, and how I could be so clueless when that's literally a question we've been asked since we were kids. Well, simply put, this is a chapter because it is *so* important to implement and if I never thought of it that way, maybe you wouldn't either. I looked at "sitting with that" as more about what I *thought* and not so much about what I *felt*. This shift changed the way I process my emotions.

When I learned to sit with myself, I realized that it wasn't just a series of stewing in my own emotions; it wasn't meant to keep me in the same emotional state. Instead, I began to work through what I was feeling. I acknowledged how I was feeling, embraced new perspectives, and asked myself how both made me feel. From there, I took it a step further and asked myself if that's how I *wanted* to feel. If it wasn't, I would take one more step and ask what I needed to do to get there. This is the work. This is the process.

My first time really putting this into action was when my father unexpectedly passed away in 2019. After the initial shock and the immediate chaos dwindled down, I felt an immense amount of guilt. I felt guilty that I was not more upset and that I didn't think of him every second of every day. I completely doused myself in shame and loathing. Was I a horrible daughter? Through therapy and coaching, I was able to process this and find a new perspective. I told my therapist that it felt as though I immediately accepted what happened and moved on, and that didn't feel right. We discussed my relationship with him, which was great, and she told me that oftentimes people have regrets when loved ones die. They feel as though they should have said or done more. They wished they had more time to make things right. With me and my father, things were already right; we had a close relationship, and my final memory was celebrating my parents' anniversary with him, my mom, and my sister. It was a true family day, one of the things he cherished most in life. With that said, my therapist gave me the perspective that maybe I came to peace with it so quickly because I was happy with our relationship and there were no regrets. That was the start of shifting my mindset and releasing the guilt.

Later on, when I began my work with Keri, my guilt was still surfacing. I felt better after therapy, but it was still lingering inside me and I just couldn't let it go. I remember so clearly having an entire session strictly about this. I could go on for pages about all the powerful things that were said that day, but I'll just share the outcome as a whole. We discussed the idea that much like any other emotion, grief is not linear. There is no right or wrong way to grieve. It was also made clear to me that no one else could tell me how to grieve. Others kept telling me that one day I would go to call him out of habit and then it would hit me. Well that never happened, and it made me feel like crap. However, all I was doing was placing their definition of grief onto myself. I wasn't wrong. I wasn't a terrible daughter. I was simply processing the way I knew how. The way my body needed to process. Of course at the end of the session she told me to sit with that and let her know what came up. I did just that and here's how it went:

How do my current emotions and views on my grief make me feel? Guilty. Sad. Ashamed. Broken. Misunderstood. Misguided. Selfish. Wrong.

How would shifting to the new 'grief is not linear' mindset make me feel? Human. Relieved. Open. Like a weight has been lifted. Happy. Connected.

How do I want to feel? I want to feel the shift. I want to feel at peace and know my father feels the same.

What do I need to do to get there? Decide. Decide that I'm going to break the patterns of what grief means to me. Decide that I'm going to release myself from the shame and the guilt and allow my feelings to be okay. Decide to remind myself of my new thought patterns everyday and to come back when they feel far away. Decide to write my father a letter and read it out loud. Decide to remember that my emotions are never wrong.

It's not easy and I'd be lying if I said the guilt never resurfaces. It certainly does. The difference is that I have the tools to work through it now. I no longer continue to feel shame and loathe myself when the feelings arise. I acknowledge, I process, and I heal a little bit more each time.

Your Turn

Think about a situation that you can't seem to put behind you. Something that continues to creep up on you. Let's work through it:

What is the situation?

____

____

____

____

____

How does it make you feel?

How do you want to feel?

What do you need to do to get there? What new perspective could you work on adopting to help?

____

____

____

____

If you're not going through anything substantial right now, bookmark this page and come back to it whenever something arises.

THE LESSON

Don't be afraid to go deeper. There are layers of yourself you have yet to even meet. The more you peel back those layers, the more you'll be able to process your emotions and heal from the inside out. Whether you're really trying and feel like you don't know how, or you're trying to brush your emotions under the rug so as to not deal with them, they aren't going away.

> Your emotions are part of you and they are part of your journey. Each time you work through them, you're one step closer to who you want to be. Sit with that and see what comes up.

Chapter 7:
Let It *Go!*

This chapter is dedicated to the ever so popular phrase: Let it go! Just let it go! If only it were that easy. I want to preface this chapter by saying that when I'm discussing letting things go here, I'm not speaking about it in a dismissive way. There's nothing worse than when you're trying to work through something and someone tells you to let it go as if it's not a big deal. What you're feeling is absolutely a big deal. What I'm talking about are those situations that you're *ready* to let go of, but don't quite know how. Every time you think you're good, you're not; am I right? Been there! Let's break down some of the most common things we as human beings want to let go of…at least in my own personal experience.

Breakups

You can't tell me this isn't the first place your mind went to when thinking about trying your damnedest to let go! There are so many things that try to knock us down in life, but nothing hurts quite like a broken heart. The never-ending tears, the anxiety in the pit of your stomach, the feeling that you will literally never be okay again…these are the worst! All painful breakups tend to feel this way in the moment, but some sting more than others. Remember that toxic breakup I mentioned in the beginning of the book? Well, that was my rock bottom in the breakup world. I was shattered from head to toe and thought I would never recover. I was so incredibly angry–both at him for how I was treated and at myself for allowing said treatment for almost two years. But you know what? Without that relationship and that breakup, I wouldn't be the woman I am today. It forced me to pick myself up and rebuild…to truly learn how to love myself and know with all my heart that I was going to be okay. In doing so, I was able to let go in a way that I never had before. Enter my two new best friends: block and purge…

Block

One of my biggest strengths when it comes to breakups is that if I tell myself I'm not going to reach out anymore, I won't. If I say I'm not going to stalk around on Instagram, I won't. I don't impulse text or drunk dial. When I'm done, I'm done–physically. Emotionally is a whole other ballgame…we'll get to that in a minute. So most recently, when I got tired of the unproductive back and forth, I told my ex that I would no longer be responding and I didn't…ever. A few months later I recognized that although I was acting as if I was in control by not engaging, I actually wasn't. He was in control because I was still reading his messages and they affected my mood and ability to move forward. That was when I knew enough was enough, and I needed to take my power back. I blocked him through every means possible. I've never had to block anyone in my life so this seemed extreme for me, but it was necessary.

> **You can stand in this type of power and self-love simply by asking yourself: is this helping or hurting me?**

Continuing to read the messages–some of which were downright nasty and degrading–and allowing him the opportunity to reach out was hurting me, so I stopped. Now, if you can honestly and authentically still communicate with an ex and/or respect each other's boundaries, you obviously do not need to take it this far. Use your judgment. However, if this is what you need to move on, then honor that. Take care of yourself!

Purge

Moving along to that pesky emotional side…the one I said I'd get back to. I certainly felt empowered by my ability to stand my ground, but that didn't make it hurt any less internally. I was still a wreck, wondering if I would ever move on and feeling guilty for blocking him. Then, at Keri's direction of course, I did something I always told myself I couldn't do: I got rid of all photos and items that reminded me of him. I'm talking about a full-blown purge. Some people may find this perfectly normal and a must-do with any breakup, but it was hard for this empath. I always felt like maybe one day I would want those memories, or what if we got back together and I had thrown everything away? I saved everything and just tucked it away figuring "out of sight, out of mind." Unfortunately that wasn't the case, and it was keeping me more attached than I realized. I can say with full confidence that tossing everything in the dumpster and deleting every picture from my phone was *liberating*. It was what kicked my moving on into high gear…and I never looked back again!

To sum up: when dealing with a breakup you just can't seem to let go of…block, delete, purge! Stand in your power and take control of your mental health.

Oh, and side note: the same method applies with friendships. I've done that too! Insert thumbs up emoji…

Your Turn

Take some time to go through your phone and delete any photos, numbers, or reminders of anyone that is no longer serving you. If the relationship has not yet ended, but you want it to, have the hard conversation. Then, come back to this section and purge! Write a few words indicating how you feel when you're done.

____

____

____

____

____

____

Mindset

In regards to mindset, I'm mainly referring to letting go of limiting beliefs and old thought patterns. They are so hard to break because most of the time these beliefs have been ingrained in us for years. There is hope though! If I had to describe the process in one word, it would be: decide. I know, I've mentioned deciding as a solution for several concepts already, but it just works for so many things! Think about your way of thinking around different concepts, situations, and/or emotions, and decide if that's what is best for you and your growth. If not, decide how you would like to reframe your thoughts and choose those thoughts every single day.

Decide even when it doesn't feel true. Then decide again. And again. And again. You get it.

Let me give you an example. As I've mentioned previously, what started this whole journey for me was my thought patterns surrounding codependency. My mindset was stuck on the notion that if I wasn't needed, I wouldn't be wanted. I felt like others' love for me was based on how much I could do for them. I deemed myself a giver, and wanted so badly to help people. Naturally, this mindset was not serving me. It made me believe I couldn't be happy without being in a relationship, and it led me to attract projects, not partners. I wondered endlessly about why I wasn't finding a partner that was on my level, one that put in as much effort as I always did. Well, my mindset was why; Law of Attraction–negativity breeds negativity. That's when I knew I had to reframe my thoughts, learn how to love myself unconditionally, and be truly happy alone. In the beginning of this revelation I was freshly going through my toxic breakup, so of course old thoughts would resurface and I would often feel lonely. Instead of wallowing in that feeling and wishing I was with someone else (or worse–back with him), I reminded myself in each moment how I wanted to feel and that I was doing these things to allow myself to heal. Following this process every time a negative thought around codependency showed up, combined with the steps written about throughout this entire book, allowed me to find my love and peace. I was intentionally single for a year and a half, and it was the happiest I had ever been. It doesn't happen overnight, but once you decide, the shift will follow.

I'll give you another example…the most important example in my opinion. Let's talk about success. I've always thought about success in two categories: financial and life in general. I grew up believing that achieving financial success was a completely textbook process: go to school, get good grades, continue to college, get more good grades, get a job, be financially stable. This was the only way. My parents never went over the top when it came to pressuring me and didn't force me into things I didn't want to do, but this was still the mindset I was raised with. Life success meant meeting "the one," getting married, having children, buying a house…the whole nine yards. It's the basic sequence of life and I just assumed that I would follow suit. Let me tell you what happened instead…

Financial

I did all the things one might expect given my upbringing. I got all the good grades, went to college, got a teaching job right after I graduated, and became more financially stable than I ever thought possible given my career choice. However, fast forward fifteen years and I seriously began contemplating a career change. Like, resigning in the next six months-type serious. This changed everything. It went against everything I knew. I couldn't possibly quit such a stable job…one that I spent years preparing for…could I? I'll be honest, I first started thinking about leaving teaching a year prior when I had what I would deem the worst school year of my entire career. I wasn't sure if I would actually follow through with leaving–hello old "it can't happen for me" mindset–so I committed to using year fifteen as my deciding year. As I mentioned when discussing revamping my affirmations in Chapter 4, I wanted to be proactive in making such an epic decision, so I hired Sarah. Together we got to the root cause of why I was so hesitant to leave: my definition of success. I felt like if I resigned, I would no longer be successful because I would no longer have that stability. In working with Sarah, I started redefining what success could mean. I reread my affirmations with this concept in mind:

- Money will continue to flow; I am meant for abundance.
- I am fulfilled in my career.
- I can find success in unexpected ways.

I wrote down different definitions of success, such as feeling at peace with my life, having more freedom, and looking forward to each day. Much like I discussed with codependency, I reminded myself of these things every time a negative thought pattern entered my mind. I also intentionally visualized what it would look and feel like to hand in my resignation. Over time, I started to really believe it could happen and that I would survive no matter what. Now, in this very moment of writing, I can proudly say I've handed in my resignation letter, invested in a course specifically designed to help teachers transition to new careers, and am getting thoroughly excited about my future. It is still one of the scariest decisions I have ever had to make, but it also felt quite freeing.

Life

If you recall, I touched extremely briefly on a twelve-year relationship back in the introduction. This was with a man I met in college who I thought would be my forever; in the beginning because we fell in love, in the end because of pure comfort. I truly thought if it wasn't him, it wasn't anyone and I was scared to be alone after all that time.

As you can probably guess, that relationship ended. Why? Many reasons, but ultimately we wanted different things for our future. He wanted children. I did not. I broke the societal norm of wanting children many years ago when I decided having my own was not for me. Now, with a breakup at the age of thirty-two, I had to redefine the whole meet someone, get married, have children, and buy a house aspect of success because even if I still wanted some of those things, it wasn't in the cards for me on the timeline I originally thought. I had to come to terms with the fact that I didn't necessarily want the things I was "supposed" to want, learn how to find peace within myself, and trust the process. I'm currently thirty-eight, with the love of my life (not engaged or married), and renting an apartment (alone) that's way overpriced, but is one that I adore. And guess what? I am beyond okay with my lifestyle. In fact, I wouldn't want it any other way.

Learning how to love and truly be with yourself can really set the foundation for accepting a whole new mindset around success.

Rather than repeat myself, I encourage you to go back to Chapter 1 (Love Yourself First) and remind yourself just how important this step is to solidify your foundation on this journey. Referring back to Chapter 4 (Affirmations) and Chapter 6 (Sit With That) can also help as both touch on ways in which you can reframe your thoughts.

Your Turn

Write down one ingrained thought pattern that you would like to change.

____

____

____

____

____

Write down the new thought pattern you would like to have.

____

____

____

____

____

Remind yourself of this new thought daily. *Decide* to make the shift.

| THE LESSON |

It all comes back to deciding. There is *so* much power in just making a decision. So, simply put:

Decide to let it go!

However that looks for you, commit to your decision. Block the number, purge the stuff, redefine your ways of thinking… stand firmly in your truth and in your power. You've got this!

Chapter 8:
Boundaries

Boundaries are such a hot topic when it comes to personal development because they are so damn important. Many people choose not to set boundaries because they can be overwhelming and uncomfortable. Boundaries need to be set both with others and yourself, and they revolve around every aspect of your life. There are three areas that I believe are the most important when starting to set new boundaries: core values, time, and energy.

Core Values

This is where you get to take a look at what truly matters to you. What are the things you value most? Your values might be simple and one-word like freedom, honesty, loyalty, authenticity, or creativity. They might be more specific like spending quality time with your family, speaking up for what you believe in, or helping others. Whatever they are for you, it's necessary to identify them so that you can be sure you're living in alignment with them. If you're not, this is where boundaries come into play. For example, if you value speaking up for what you believe in, but you don't share your thoughts with certain people when something is wrong, you're not living in alignment. You can set a boundary here that you will no longer surround yourself with people that shut you down. You will only surround yourself with people who lift you up and those who you trust and feel comfortable speaking up to when necessary.

Core values bleed into time and energy because those elements themselves may be two of your core values. Even so, it's extremely beneficial to take a look at your specific values first and really get clear on what's important to you personally. This is a great way to go deep and get to know yourself better.

Your Turn

List some of your core values. If you've never thought about this before and are having some trouble, do a quick search on core values and see what resonates with you.

____

____

____

____

____

Time

How many times have you felt overworked or as if there are not enough hours in the day? I know I've felt this way too many times to count. We live in a world where we often feel forced to go, go, go and we don't take a moment to slow down or really look at how our time is being spent. Depending on your job, you might have set working hours with tasks that have to be completed, but for the rest of the day you get to choose how you spend your time. Boundaries here can fall into three subcategories: personal, loved ones, and career.

Personal

How much time do you actually spend with yourself? Are you taking care of yourself and your mental health? I sure hope so, but if you're not, I encourage you to start after reading this book. When I was single and working on myself, I spent every waking second with, well…me! I had all the personal time in the world and I loved it. Not only did I do tons of self-care activities, but it was also easier to get back on track if I fell out of alignment for a bit. When I started dating my boyfriend, I had to begin setting boundaries around personal time. Naturally I wanted to spend endless quality time with him, but I didn't want to lose myself in the process. Luckily, he was nothing but supportive and wanted the same for himself. Sure, we still fall off sometimes and make plans when we could have personal time or don't use the personal time we allotted as intended, but we have boundaries in place that allow us to freely share, without judgment, when we want alone time. I also have a personal boundary that I will work on my growth (beyond my daily routines) at least once a week. I frequently do it more, but this helps ensure that I don't step out of alignment as often.

It's also crucial to have boundaries within boundaries. For instance, I have the boundary just mentioned where I will work on my personal growth at least once per week. I then have to make even more specific boundaries to help make that time more productive. One of my favorite personal growth tasks has been writing this book. When doing so, I set a boundary that while writing I won't check my phone for thirty minutes at a time. This lessens the distraction of mindless scrolling.

Loved Ones

Setting boundaries with loved ones–family, friends, significant others–is a more difficult task because you probably don't want to hurt anyone's feelings. If you're an empath like me, it might be really hard for you to say no or allocate your time if someone needs you or asks for a favor. Keep in mind that it is okay to not want to do something…to say no when it doesn't feel right…to advocate for yourself if you feel like you're being taken advantage of frequently. There are certain people who–intentionally or unintentionally–will disrespect your time because they know that you'll be there. When you know they are unaware of what they are doing, it becomes even harder to say no.

Back before I had any boundaries around my time, I had a friend who would ask for favors often. She would ask for some ridiculous things that essentially wasted time I could have used more efficiently had I set some boundaries in the first place. I just always said yes, even if I didn't want to, because "that's just what friends do." I didn't realize it at the time, but she was taking advantage of the fact that she knew she could always count on me to comply. Now, just to be clear, of course it is perfectly acceptable to ask for whatever you need (no matter how ridiculous), especially with your closest friends. My dad always said, "It never hurts to ask!" However, those favors should be reciprocated–not in an "I'll do this if you do that" kind of way, but rather there should be an understanding that you'll both be there for each other. Unfortunately in my case, when I would ask for something, I'd often be met with a hard no if it was of any inconvenience to her. That's where the disconnect happened.

There should be no such phrase as "that's just what friends do." There's a strong difference between being a good friend and helping others out–even when you don't want to sometimes–and allowing someone to take advantage of your kindness. More recently, I had a different friend become stranded at an airport because her ride could no longer pick her up. She was hesitant to even ask and she could have taken an Uber or taxi, but I offered to go get her. The night prior I barely got any sleep because I woke up early to watch the sunrise, and her flight wasn't coming in until late so I wouldn't actually get back home until after midnight. Did I want to drive over two hours round trip when I was utterly exhausted? No. But… did I feel taken advantage of? Also no. I may have preferred not to do the physical task at hand, but what I did want to do was help my friend who was unexpectedly in a tough spot. Our friendship was genuine enough to make me feel like I *wanted* to help, not like I *had* to help simply because that's what friends do. That's the difference.

When it comes to your loved ones, evaluate how much time is being spent doing things because you want to and it's quality time, versus how much time is being spent simply so you don't feel guilty. Guilt is such a big emotion and it has its time and place, but it doesn't belong in the realm of setting boundaries. Doing what's best for you while keeping your integrity and alignment with the person you want to be is never selfish. It's an act of self-love and it is necessary.

The people who support your growth and are meant to be in your life will not only understand your need to set boundaries, but also encourage it!

Career

This one is a biggie. Depending on your job, it may take up the majority of your day. It may even take up some of your evenings. For me, being a teacher meant being expected to go above and beyond, even when the time to do so was rarely given. At the preschool grade level, this involved setting up the classroom each morning, lesson planning, data analysis, assessments, evaluation paperwork, messaging families, creating a weekly newsletter, meetings, and more…all designated to fit into approximately sixty-five "extra" minutes per day. It simply was not enough to get it all done and many teachers ended up coming in early, staying late, or taking their work home. I decided to set boundaries around this premise a long time ago. I also continued to set new ones each year. I only came in early or stayed late if I genuinely wanted to because it felt good to me to have that extra time, and I stopped taking work home on a regular basis. I had job duties and I had set hours. As long as I was using my time efficiently, there was only so much I could do. Somehow, the important stuff always seemed to get done so I stopped stressing. The most recent boundary I set was to not volunteer for additional tasks or events I didn't have the time or mental bandwidth for. Much like I discussed in regards to time with loved ones, there is a huge difference between feeling passionate about a project or wanting to help out the community and feeling expected to do so (something I felt for many years). If you are not required to do anything outside of your job description and daily duties, then you hold the power to allocate your time how you see fit and not feel bad about it.

Energy

This section could be written in just three words: protect your energy.

Your energy is your most valuable asset, and you need to treat it as such. When I think of my energy, I directly correlate it to my mental health. If I feel drained, depleted, confused, or just out of alignment, I'm generally stressed and my mental health is suffering in some way. If I feel excited, content, at peace, and in alignment, my mental health is usually high-vibe.

Naturally there are going to be ebbs and flows in life. It can't be rainbows and butterflies all of the time. We all go through rough seasons where it feels like we just can't get back into a good place. Being intentional about protecting your energy helps to better navigate and not add to these seasons.

Anything or anyone that is draining your energy *needs* to go!

Of course it's much easier said than done depending on the situation. There may need to be actions put into place to get to your final outcome. If your job is making you miserable, you may not be able to just up and quit. What you can do is look at what steps you can take to make it more manageable while you plan for your future. What changes can you make throughout your day to make it less stressful? What do you have to do in order to feel comfortable quitting? Or maybe there's a romantic relationship or friendship that's been feeling off. If you feel as though it's reached its peak, go ahead and end it. If you feel it's worth trying to save, think about the conversation you can have with that person and what you can do to make it better.

Even something as simple as everyday routines can affect your energy. There's no benefit to doing things just to do them. They have to be done with intention and embodiment. When I first started my journey, I journaled every single morning. I used the guided journals mentioned in previous chapters which were great, but eventually journaling felt mundane. I continued doing it because I thought that's what I had to do in order to heal, but I wasn't getting anything out of it anymore. It felt like a chore—and if you recall, it should absolutely *not* feel this way. So I stopped and wouldn't you know, I continued healing.

> **You do not have to do what you've always done.**
> **You do not have to be who you've always been.**
> **This is your permission to evolve.**

Your Turn

Much like anything else, if you try to set boundaries in all areas of your life at once, you'll most likely end up overwhelmed. Work on one area at a time.

In what area of your life would you like to start setting some more boundaries? If you choose time, be specific in which subcategory you want to start with.

Write down three boundaries you can set within that area.

Choose the one that feels most in alignment with your current goal and start there. Keep the other two in mind as you progress and begin to set more.

BONUS

Here are some specific examples of boundaries you can set to get started if you're struggling to come up with your own. Use them as they are, or tweak them to fit your needs.

Core Values:

- I will express myself to my significant other when something is bothering me.
- I will only associate with people who are honest with me and I will be honest with them.
- I will follow through on my word to myself.

Time:

- I will put my phone on do not disturb at 9:30pm and not look at it for the rest of the night.
- I will say no to my family when something feels out of alignment, and I will not feel guilty about it.
- I will leave work no later than fifteen minutes past my end time.

Energy:

- I will surround myself with people who lift me up and encourage my growth.
- I will start each day with gratitude.
- I will plan for "me time" once per week.

| THE LESSON |

Boundaries are a lot like affirmations and even more like habits. They get stronger with practice. You might not get it exactly right the first few times; you might even disregard them and fall back into old patterns because of guilt or comfort. Even when this happens, continue to maintain them as much as possible and you'll start to see a shift…in your mindset, your quality of life, and your overall way of being.

Remember, "no" is a complete sentence…and taking care of yourself is not selfish!

How to Navigate Guilt

I wanted to add a quick excerpt here about how I actually navigate guilt when it comes to saying no. Whenever I'm working on something unfamiliar, my first question is "how do I do that?" I'm a person who wants action steps, but unfortunately it doesn't always work that way when it comes to personal development. There are many coaches, mentors, and books out there that can offer a more in-depth protocol for better navigating guilt, but here's what I do. Hopefully it will help you too.

Whenever I'm in a situation where guilt is weighing on me, I think about my decision and why I chose what I did. Whether I declined an invitation, said no to a favor that was asked of me, chose not to participate in a work activity, or just flat out didn't want to do something, I remember my why. Next, I think about my actions and intentions. Did I act with integrity? Was I respectful toward the other person? Am I saying no to protect my boundaries and stay in alignment, rather than out of spite and bitterness? If I answer yes to all of these questions and know that I can put my head on my pillow at night feeling like I remain a good person, I'm able to release the guilt.

We are all human and we are going to make mistakes. If you answer no to any of these questions and truly feel like you want to change your mind, you can do so with grace. If the people you're interacting with are genuine and meant to be in your life, they'll understand and appreciate your honesty.

Chapter 9: Move Your Body

This is a shorter chapter and is mainly here to serve as a reminder. I was into health and fitness even before I embarked on my personal development journey. Since movement can literally be medicine (and actually is for me) I just couldn't leave it out of this book. The reason it's shorter is because there isn't much to say about moving your body other than: do it! In the interest of not being preachy, let's dig a little deeper.

There are endless studies and articles you can read about the positive effects of movement and exercise, but this book is intended to be more conversational and relatable, so I don't want to reiterate said studies. What I do want to share is the power movement holds for me and how you can incorporate it into your life if you're not already. For those of you who love movement and exercise, kudos to you. You can probably skip this chapter entirely and keep doing what you're doing. For those of you who don't do it often, don't really think about it much, or downright despise it…you're not alone. Keep reading.

The How

First and foremost, I truly believe that exercise should not be viewed as a punishment. The mindset of *having* to work out in order to reach a specific goal is going to make it seem more daunting. Instead, view it as *getting* to move your body to keep it active and healthy. We only get one body, so why not take care of it? Of course if you have a goal of toning up, losing weight, or increasing stamina, you're going to have to put in the work. It won't just happen because you made the choice to be healthy. What this shift in mindset does is help to eliminate the dread people often associate with exercise.

Another key way to get started and stick with it is to find something you enjoy. You may think that there's no workout you would like, but that's probably not true. Movement and exercise can include anything from taking a walk to dancing to weightlifting to yoga and beyond. There are so many options, there's bound to be something that sparks your interest. You can even choose if you prefer high or low-impact. There are cheaper gyms you can join, at-home workout programs (my personal favorite), and tons of free *YouTube* videos. In doing some trial and error, I have found that I love completing programs where I have a start and end date, calendar of workouts, and trainer on my television. As far as style, kickboxing is my favorite but I also love programs that combine cardio and weightlifting. Having the start and end date keeps me motivated, disciplined, and on track because I know I'm working toward something specific. It also gives me an immense sense of accomplishment each time I finish a program. Call me crazy, but I get emotional with every new program I complete!

When you're looking for something, be sure to keep an open mind. Although it's not my favorite means of movement, I was shocked to see what a barre workout really was like. It was low-impact, but hard! I went into it thinking I would hate it and it turned out to be very fun and enjoyable. Oftentimes we have a picture of what something will be in our minds, and that closes us off from even wanting to try. Do a sample workout and you just might be surprised.

Lastly, if this isn't something that comes naturally to you, start small. Doing too much too soon could lead to overwhelm and a sense of failure. Instead of initially making a goal to workout six times a week for an hour each day, start with three times a week for twenty minutes. This will help keep you on track and give you ample time to find what you enjoy, without feeling pressured. Once you're in a good spot, you can increase to four or five times per week. Eventually, you'll be a pro and forget why you hated it in the first place!

The Why

Obviously staying healthy is the number one priority here.

It goes without saying that we all want to be and remain the best versions of ourselves, and we can't do that if we're not moving.

We are not meant to be sedentary beings. If you're a research-oriented person, search for some of those aforementioned articles to really learn how moving your body can enhance your health and quality of life.

Aside from overall health, moving my body regularly lifts my mood. It truly changes the way I feel at any given moment. Even when I don't want to do it, the adrenaline rush after is never regretted. It is also a wonderful outlet when my stress levels are high or my mental health is suffering.

Movement gives me: joy, strength, a sense of accomplishment, a release, discipline, power, pride, purpose, and so much more.

I have found that exercising in the morning works best for me. When I started doing morning workouts, it changed my mood for the entire day. I felt more energized and ready to take on my job. It made my mornings happier and I actually looked forward to waking up early to get my workout in first thing. I used to exercise after work and would often find myself tired and sluggish, sitting on the couch too long and not wanting to get it done. It led me to that mindset of *having* to work out instead of *wanting* to, and I didn't like that so I switched it up. I say this so that if you try something out and you don't find it enhancing your life, do it in a different way. Don't give up.

Your Turn

What are some forms of movement and exercise you think you might enjoy (i.e. walking, running, strength training, dancing, yoga, pilates, barre…)?

____

____

____

____

____

If you chose something beyond walking or running, take some time to look for more information and videos about those types of workouts. Try a sample workout and see how it feels. Start exploring what you like!

| THE LESSON |

Move your body. That's it! Get up and move. A body in motion is a body that's thriving.

Final Thoughts

Congrats! You did it! You took a giant step toward bettering yourself and that deserves a huge celebration!

Now that you've reached the end of this book, it's time to decide what resonates with you most...what feels most aligned with the steps you want to take to become the next version of yourself. Every single one of these practices have shaped who I am as a woman, and they can do the same for you if you allow it. At the end of the day, it all comes down to trust: trusting the Universe, God, Source, Spirit–whatever you choose to believe in–but most importantly, trusting *yourself*... the one thing we should all agree to believe in.

Trusting yourself might be one of the hardest things to achieve; I still struggle to this day. We live in a world filled with so many different choices that we fear making the wrong one. Here's the thing...no one knows you like you do. No one has the answers like you do. No one else is you but you. You were put on this earth for a purpose and if you are feeling like there's more, it's because there is. You wouldn't have a desire if it wasn't available for you. Trust that!

Before you close this book for good, I encourage you to go back and reread any sections that truly spoke to you. Reread anything you may have underlined or highlighted. Reread your answers to the prompts. Complete any prompts you may have skipped. The most important thing right now is embodiment;

you certainly don't have to do everything, but you need to do something. What small step can you take to move closer to who you want to be? Simply closing this book and putting it on the shelf is not the answer.

Remember, you're already there…right where you're meant to be. You've asked for guidance and here it is, but it's all already inside of you. You have everything you'll ever need.

YOU are the Vibe!

BONUS:
Lessons Learned

I wanted to add a little pocket guide of some of the greatest lessons I've learned throughout my journey, ones that I hope you will benefit from too as you implement what you've learned from this book. Flip back to this section when you need a reminder of why you chose this path or just a quick hit of inspiration.

Start with your foundation. Build the relationship you have with yourself. Love yourself first and everything else will fall into place.

Happiness is a choice and you get to choose it every single day. Having an overall sense of joy surrounding your life will help you through the tough seasons. Happiness is healing. Evolving. Chasing your dreams. Surrounding yourself with people who lift you up. Dancing. Being your authentic self. Happiness is not all external…it's an inside job.

Go to therapy. Hire the coach. Take the course. Start the business. Write the book. You'll never regret investing in yourself and it will change your life for the better.

Don't sweat the times you weren't your best self or accepted something well below what you deserved. You get to raise the bar for yourself. You may hit rock bottom again on this journey, but your rock bottom won't be as far down. – Words of wisdom from Keri during one of our very first coaching sessions.

Don't just read your affirmations; embody them. Visualize the person you want to be. Act as if you're already there.

Settling—in life and love—is no longer an option.

There is so much power in just deciding.

To quote Keri yet again, "What got you here won't get you there." Growth is a never-ending process. Keep evolving.

Every situation—positive and negative—is feedback. Be open to receiving the lesson. Things don't always go according to plan. Whatever is meant for you will find its way to you.

If you remove one phrase from your repertoire, let it be "It is what it is." It is NOT what it is. It gets to be whatever you make it. It gets to change right along with you. You are not meant to stay stagnant. It is not "just the way you are." Never underestimate reintroducing yourself to the world.

Confidence is not just physical—it's mental and emotional. It's a mindset that comes back to healing and trusting yourself. Confidence is being unapologetically you in all aspects of your life.

Be grateful for even the smallest of things. The small wins are just as important as the big ones. The small steps often lead to the biggest steps.

Allow yourself to truly feel. Don't be ashamed or hide. There is nothing wrong with you. Emotions are not linear.

Boundaries are not selfish; they are necessary.

This process will hurt. It will be uncomfortable. You'll feel like you've failed. You'll get knocked down. But you'll also get back up… and you'll be even stronger. You'll step into your power and move forward toward the person you're meant to be.

You can't have the light without the dark. The dark often makes the light shine brighter. Keep your heart and mind open. Duality always.

Shameless Plug

- If you enjoyed this book and would like to stay connected, I'd love for you to follow me on Instagram where I continuously share nuggets of inspiration to help you heal, grow, and change your life. I also have those epic dance parties!

  ⬡ : @sheis_ericamarie

- If you feel called to share this book with others, it would mean the absolute world to me. Just you being here makes my heart happy and the thought of my words reaching even more people brings me so much joy.

  Thank you!

Resources & Recommendations

Here you'll find a list of resources mentioned in the book, as well as recommendations for others you may find helpful. These have all been incredible for my healing and growth.

Books

Atomic Habits by James Clear
Fear Is My Homeboy by Judi Holler
Girl, Wash Your Face by Rachel Hollis
*The Life-Changing Magic of Not Giving a F*CK* by Sarah Knight
You Are A Badass by Jen Sincero

Journals

Gratitude: A Day and Night Reflection Journal by Insight Editions
Mindful Makeover by Stephanie Robilio
True You by Kelly Vincent

Podcasts

Aligned Woman Podcast with Keri Kugler
*Her Best F***ing Life* with Sarah Ordo
Style Your Mind with Cara Alwill

The Freely YOU Podcast with Sarah Heredia
Yes, And with Judi Holler

Spiritual

If you're ready to explore some spiritual guidance, I highly recommend the book *Light Is the New Black* by Rebecca Campbell, as well as her Work Your Light Oracle Cards.

Acknowledgements

First, a huge thank you to my sister, Pam. Thank you for always being my rock. You have been by my side for all of the good times and bad, the breakups and makeups, the friendships gained and lost, and my evolution as a woman. You have supported every step of my journey from day one and I truly don't know what I would do or where I would be without you. I appreciate your endless advice and the many times you've talked me out of a pickle. You're the best sister a girl could ask for!

Second, to my amazing boyfriend, John. There is no way I could have written this book without your infinite support and encouragement. I can't thank you enough for allowing me to be giddy with excitement, filled with imposter syndrome, and everything in between. Your belief in me and my dream never faltered and I am forever grateful. Thank you for loving me through it all!

Next, to the extraordinary Keri Kugler, the driving force behind my growth. Thank you for coming into my life when you did. Thank you for always having faith that it's all possible for me. Thank you for being an incredible source of inspiration daily. Thank you for writing the foreword for this book. Thank you for being my coach, my mentor, my friend, and one of my biggest cheerleaders.

To the phenomenal team of people that helped make this book a reality: Emily Arthur, Michael Boalch, and Sarah Heredia. Emily, you had such a great way of editing my work while keeping my voice and message intact. Thank you for being patient with me, taking the time to answer all of my questions, and understanding my complete lack of deadlines. You helped bring my book to life and it means the absolute world to me. Michael, you took a mere vision in my mind and turned it into the most beautiful cover. Thank you for all of the hard work and tweaks it took to make it perfect. Another big thank you for your expertise with formatting. It gave the interior its own vibe and made the process of publishing so much smoother. Sarah, thank you for taking the time to do a beta read and provide feedback. I'm so lucky to have crossed paths with you and our work together was what lit a fire under me to make the big, scary changes. Keep spreading your light in this world!

Thank you to the many family, friends, acquaintances, and strangers who offered their excitement and said they can't wait to read this before it was even finished…to those who congratulated me and gave words of encouragement throughout the process. You are appreciated!

To you–my wonderful readers. There are no words to describe what I feel when I think about you choosing my book as you embark on a journey of your own. My goal has always been and always will be to inspire others to step into their power and believe it *can* happen for them. I hope that's what you've taken from my book. Thank you, from the bottom of my heart, for trusting me to guide you. And always remember, YOU are the Vibe!

Last, but certainly not least, to Mom & Dad. I love you!